50 Premium Ice Cream Cake Recipes

By: Kelly Johnson

Table of Contents

- Chocolate Fudge Swirl Ice Cream Cake
- Classic Vanilla Bean Ice Cream Cake
- Strawberry Cheesecake Ice Cream Cake
- Cookies and Cream Dream Cake
- Mint Chocolate Chip Ice Cream Cake
- Mocha Espresso Ice Cream Cake
- Lemon Meringue Ice Cream Cake
- Peanut Butter Cup Ice Cream Cake
- Red Velvet Ice Cream Cake
- S'mores Ice Cream Cake
- Neapolitan Ice Cream Cake
- Tiramisu Ice Cream Cake
- Caramel Pecan Ice Cream Cake
- Rocky Road Ice Cream Cake
- Coconut Cream Pie Ice Cream Cake
- Salted Caramel Brownie Ice Cream Cake
- Pumpkin Spice Ice Cream Cake
- Chocolate Hazelnut Ice Cream Cake
- Dulce de Leche Ice Cream Cake
- Apple Pie Ice Cream Cake
- Blueberry Cheesecake Ice Cream Cake
- Chocolate Mint Chip Ice Cream Cake
- Almond Joy Ice Cream Cake
- Pina Colada Ice Cream Cake
- Raspberry Truffle Ice Cream Cake
- Tiramisu Ice Cream Cake with Espresso Crunch
- Lemon Blueberry Ice Cream Cake
- Birthday Cake Ice Cream Cake
- Chocolate Raspberry Ice Cream Cake
- Coffee Toffee Ice Cream Cake
- Peanut Butter Banana Ice Cream Cake
- Pistachio Almond Ice Cream Cake
- Chocolate Cherry Ice Cream Cake
- Mango Coconut Ice Cream Cake
- Key Lime Pie Ice Cream Cake

- Nutella Hazelnut Ice Cream Cake
- Oreo Truffle Ice Cream Cake
- Maple Pecan Ice Cream Cake
- Banana Foster Ice Cream Cake
- Chocolate Chip Cookie Dough Ice Cream Cake
- Chocolate Coconut Ice Cream Cake
- Cherry Almond Ice Cream Cake
- Carrot Cake Ice Cream Cake
- Cookies and Caramel Ice Cream Cake
- Tropical Paradise Ice Cream Cake
- Triple Chocolate Ice Cream Cake
- Vanilla Almond Crunch Ice Cream Cake
- Raspberry Lemonade Ice Cream Cake
- Mocha Hazelnut Ice Cream Cake
- Chocolate-Covered Strawberry Ice Cream Cake

Chocolate Fudge Swirl Ice Cream Cake

Ingredients:

- 1 pint chocolate ice cream
- 1 pint vanilla ice cream
- 1/2 cup fudge sauce (store-bought or homemade)
- 1 1/2 cups chocolate wafer cookies (or chocolate cake crumbs)
- 1/4 cup unsalted butter, melted
- 1/2 cup whipped cream (for topping)
- 1/4 cup chocolate chips (optional, for garnish)

Instructions:

1. **Prepare the crust**: Crush the chocolate wafer cookies into fine crumbs. Mix the crumbs with melted butter until evenly combined. Press the mixture into the base of a springform pan or cake pan (9-inch works well), creating a solid crust. Freeze for 15-20 minutes.
2. **Layer ice cream**: Let the chocolate and vanilla ice creams soften slightly at room temperature. Once the crust is firm, spread a layer of chocolate ice cream over the crust. Add a generous swirl of fudge sauce, then top with a layer of vanilla ice cream. Repeat if necessary for more layers.
3. **Freeze**: Once all layers are assembled, swirl in more fudge sauce and smooth the top. Cover with plastic wrap and freeze for at least 4 hours or overnight.
4. **Serve**: Before serving, top with whipped cream and chocolate chips if desired.

Classic Vanilla Bean Ice Cream Cake

Ingredients:

- 1 pint vanilla bean ice cream
- 1 pint chocolate ice cream
- 2 cups chocolate cake crumbs (from baked cake or cake mix)
- 1/4 cup butter, melted
- 1 cup whipped cream
- 1/4 cup chocolate syrup (optional for drizzling)

Instructions:

1. **Make the crust**: Combine the chocolate cake crumbs with melted butter. Press the mixture into the bottom of a 9-inch round springform pan. Freeze for 15-20 minutes.
2. **Layer ice cream**: Let the vanilla and chocolate ice creams soften for easier spreading. Spread a layer of vanilla bean ice cream over the crust, then top with a layer of chocolate ice cream. You can alternate the layers for a striped effect.
3. **Freeze**: Once both ice creams are layered, smooth the top and freeze the cake for at least 4 hours or overnight.
4. **Serve**: When ready to serve, top with whipped cream and drizzle with chocolate syrup if desired.

Strawberry Cheesecake Ice Cream Cake

Ingredients:

- 1 pint strawberry ice cream
- 1 pint cheesecake-flavored ice cream
- 1 1/2 cups graham cracker crumbs
- 1/4 cup unsalted butter, melted
- 1/2 cup strawberry sauce or puree
- Fresh strawberries (optional for garnish)

Instructions:

1. **Prepare the crust**: Mix graham cracker crumbs and melted butter until combined. Press into the base of a 9-inch springform pan. Freeze for 15-20 minutes to set.
2. **Layer ice cream**: Let the strawberry and cheesecake ice creams soften slightly. Spread the cheesecake ice cream over the crust first, followed by the strawberry ice cream. Optionally, swirl strawberry sauce through the ice cream layers for a marbled effect.
3. **Freeze**: Smooth the top, cover with plastic wrap, and freeze for at least 4 hours or until firm.
4. **Serve**: Before serving, drizzle with additional strawberry sauce and garnish with fresh strawberries.

Cookies and Cream Dream Cake

Ingredients:

- 1 pint cookies and cream ice cream
- 1 pint vanilla ice cream
- 2 cups crushed chocolate sandwich cookies
- 1/4 cup unsalted butter, melted
- 1 cup whipped cream
- 1/4 cup chocolate syrup (optional)

Instructions:

1. **Prepare the crust**: Crush the chocolate sandwich cookies and mix with melted butter. Press the mixture into the bottom of a 9-inch springform pan. Freeze for 15-20 minutes.
2. **Layer ice cream**: Let the cookies and cream and vanilla ice creams soften slightly. Spread a layer of cookies and cream ice cream over the crust, then top with a layer of vanilla ice cream.
3. **Freeze**: Smooth the top and freeze the cake for at least 4 hours or overnight.
4. **Serve**: Before serving, top with whipped cream and drizzle with chocolate syrup if desired.

Mint Chocolate Chip Ice Cream Cake

Ingredients:

- 1 pint mint chocolate chip ice cream
- 1 pint chocolate ice cream
- 1 1/2 cups chocolate wafer cookies or crumbs
- 1/4 cup unsalted butter, melted
- 1/2 cup whipped cream
- 1/4 cup mini chocolate chips (optional for garnish)

Instructions:

1. **Make the crust**: Combine chocolate wafer crumbs with melted butter and press into the base of a 9-inch springform pan. Freeze for 15-20 minutes to set.
2. **Layer ice cream**: Let both the mint chocolate chip and chocolate ice creams soften. Spread the mint chocolate chip ice cream over the crust, then top with a layer of chocolate ice cream.
3. **Freeze**: Smooth the top and freeze for at least 4 hours or overnight.
4. **Serve**: Before serving, top with whipped cream and sprinkle mini chocolate chips on top.

Mocha Espresso Ice Cream Cake

Ingredients:

- 1 pint coffee ice cream
- 1 pint chocolate ice cream
- 2 cups chocolate cookie crumbs
- 1/4 cup unsalted butter, melted
- 1/2 cup whipped cream
- 2 tablespoons espresso powder (optional for extra flavor)

Instructions:

1. **Prepare the crust**: Mix the chocolate cookie crumbs with melted butter and press into the bottom of a 9-inch springform pan. Freeze for 15-20 minutes.
2. **Layer ice cream**: Let the coffee and chocolate ice creams soften slightly. Spread a layer of coffee ice cream over the crust, followed by a layer of chocolate ice cream.
3. **Freeze**: Smooth the top and freeze the cake for at least 4 hours or overnight.
4. **Serve**: Top with whipped cream and sprinkle with espresso powder if desired.

Lemon Meringue Ice Cream Cake

Ingredients:

- 1 pint lemon ice cream
- 1 pint vanilla ice cream
- 1 1/2 cups graham cracker crumbs
- 1/4 cup unsalted butter, melted
- 1 cup whipped cream
- 1/4 cup lemon curd (optional)
- Toasted meringue (optional for topping)

Instructions:

1. **Make the crust**: Combine graham cracker crumbs and melted butter, then press into the bottom of a 9-inch springform pan. Freeze for 15-20 minutes.
2. **Layer ice cream**: Let the lemon and vanilla ice creams soften slightly. Spread a layer of lemon ice cream over the crust, followed by a layer of vanilla ice cream.
3. **Freeze**: Smooth the top and freeze for at least 4 hours or overnight.
4. **Serve**: Top with whipped cream, drizzle with lemon curd, and toast the meringue if desired.

Peanut Butter Cup Ice Cream Cake

Ingredients:

- 1 pint peanut butter ice cream
- 1 pint chocolate ice cream
- 1 1/2 cups crushed peanut butter cups
- 1/4 cup unsalted butter, melted
- 1 cup whipped cream
- 1/4 cup peanut butter sauce (optional)

Instructions:

1. **Prepare the crust**: Combine crushed peanut butter cups with melted butter and press into the bottom of a 9-inch springform pan. Freeze for 15-20 minutes.
2. **Layer ice cream**: Let the peanut butter and chocolate ice creams soften. Spread a layer of peanut butter ice cream over the crust, followed by a layer of chocolate ice cream.
3. **Freeze**: Smooth the top and freeze for at least 4 hours or overnight.
4. **Serve**: Top with whipped cream and drizzle with peanut butter sauce if desired.

Red Velvet Ice Cream Cake

Ingredients:

- 1 pint red velvet cake-flavored ice cream
- 1 pint vanilla ice cream
- 1 1/2 cups red velvet cake crumbs
- 1/4 cup unsalted butter, melted
- 1 cup whipped cream
- 1/4 cup cream cheese frosting (optional)

Instructions:

1. **Make the crust**: Combine red velvet cake crumbs with melted butter and press into the bottom of a 9-inch springform pan. Freeze for 15-20 minutes.
2. **Layer ice cream**: Let the red velvet and vanilla ice creams soften. Spread a layer of red velvet cake-flavored ice cream over the crust, followed by a layer of vanilla ice cream.
3. **Freeze**: Smooth the top and freeze for at least 4 hours or overnight.
4. **Serve**: Top with whipped cream and cream cheese frosting if desired.

S'mores Ice Cream Cake

Ingredients:

- 1 pint s'mores ice cream
- 1 pint vanilla ice cream
- 1 1/2 cups graham cracker crumbs
- 1/4 cup unsalted butter, melted
- 1 cup mini marshmallows
- 1/4 cup chocolate chips (optional for garnish)

Instructions:

1. **Prepare the crust**: Mix graham cracker crumbs with melted butter and press into the bottom of a 9-inch springform pan. Freeze for 15-20 minutes.
2. **Layer ice cream**: Let the s'mores and vanilla ice creams soften. Spread a layer of s'mores ice cream over the crust, followed by a layer of vanilla ice cream.
3. **Freeze**: Smooth the top and freeze for at least 4 hours or overnight.
4. **Serve**: Top with mini marshmallows, chocolate chips, and a drizzle of chocolate syrup if desired.

Neapolitan Ice Cream Cake

Ingredients:

- 1 pint chocolate ice cream
- 1 pint strawberry ice cream
- 1 pint vanilla ice cream
- 2 cups chocolate wafer crumbs
- 1/4 cup unsalted butter, melted
- 1/2 cup whipped cream
- Fresh strawberries (optional for garnish)

Instructions:

1. **Make the crust**: Combine chocolate wafer crumbs with melted butter and press into the bottom of a 9-inch springform pan. Freeze for 15-20 minutes.
2. **Layer ice cream**: Let the chocolate, strawberry, and vanilla ice creams soften. Spread layers of each flavor, alternating to create a Neapolitan effect.
3. **Freeze**: Smooth the top and freeze for at least 4 hours or overnight.
4. **Serve**: Top with whipped cream and fresh strawberries if desired.

Tiramisu Ice Cream Cake

Ingredients:

- 1 pint coffee ice cream
- 1 pint mascarpone or vanilla ice cream
- 1 1/2 cups ladyfinger cookies
- 1/4 cup unsalted butter, melted
- 1/2 cup whipped cream
- 2 tablespoons cocoa powder (optional for dusting)

Instructions:

1. **Prepare the crust**: Crush the ladyfinger cookies and mix with melted butter. Press into the bottom of a 9-inch springform pan. Freeze for 15-20 minutes.
2. **Layer ice cream**: Let the coffee and mascarpone ice creams soften. Spread a layer of coffee ice cream over the crust, followed by a layer of mascarpone ice cream.
3. **Freeze**: Smooth the top and freeze for at least 4 hours or overnight.
4. **Serve**: Top with whipped cream and dust with cocoa powder before serving.

Caramel Pecan Ice Cream Cake

Ingredients:

- 1 pint caramel ice cream
- 1 pint vanilla ice cream
- 1 1/2 cups pecans, chopped
- 1/4 cup unsalted butter, melted
- 1/2 cup whipped cream
- 1/4 cup caramel sauce (optional for drizzling)

Instructions:

1. **Prepare the crust**: Mix chopped pecans with melted butter and press into the bottom of a 9-inch springform pan. Freeze for 15-20 minutes.
2. **Layer ice cream**: Let the caramel and vanilla ice creams soften. Spread a layer of caramel ice cream over the crust, followed by a layer of vanilla ice cream.
3. **Freeze**: Smooth the top and freeze for at least 4 hours or overnight.
4. **Serve**: Top with whipped cream and drizzle with caramel sauce if desired.

Rocky Road Ice Cream Cake

Ingredients:

- 1 pint rocky road ice cream
- 1 pint vanilla ice cream
- 1 1/2 cups crushed graham crackers
- 1/4 cup unsalted butter, melted
- 1 cup mini marshmallows
- 1/2 cup chopped walnuts or almonds
- 1/4 cup chocolate syrup (optional)

Instructions:

1. **Prepare the crust**: Mix crushed graham crackers with melted butter and press into the bottom of a 9-inch springform pan. Freeze for 15-20 minutes.
2. **Layer ice cream**: Let the rocky road and vanilla ice creams soften. Spread a layer of rocky road ice cream over the crust, followed by a layer of vanilla ice cream.
3. **Add mix-ins**: Sprinkle mini marshmallows and chopped nuts over the ice cream layers.
4. **Freeze**: Smooth the top and freeze for at least 4 hours or overnight.
5. **Serve**: Drizzle with chocolate syrup before serving if desired.

Coconut Cream Pie Ice Cream Cake

Ingredients:

- 1 pint coconut ice cream
- 1 pint vanilla ice cream
- 1 1/2 cups graham cracker crumbs
- 1/4 cup unsalted butter, melted
- 1 cup shredded coconut
- 1/2 cup whipped cream
- 1/4 cup coconut milk (optional for drizzling)

Instructions:

1. **Prepare the crust**: Combine graham cracker crumbs with melted butter and press into the bottom of a 9-inch springform pan. Freeze for 15-20 minutes.
2. **Layer ice cream**: Let the coconut and vanilla ice creams soften. Spread a layer of coconut ice cream over the crust, followed by a layer of vanilla ice cream.
3. **Freeze**: Smooth the top and freeze for at least 4 hours or overnight.
4. **Serve**: Top with whipped cream and sprinkle with shredded coconut. Drizzle with coconut milk for extra coconut flavor.

Salted Caramel Brownie Ice Cream Cake

Ingredients:

- 1 pint salted caramel ice cream
- 1 pint chocolate brownie ice cream
- 1 1/2 cups brownie pieces (store-bought or homemade)
- 1/4 cup unsalted butter, melted
- 1/2 cup caramel sauce
- 1/2 cup whipped cream
- Sea salt (for garnish)

Instructions:

1. **Make the crust**: Mix brownie pieces with melted butter and press into the bottom of a 9-inch springform pan. Freeze for 15-20 minutes.
2. **Layer ice cream**: Let the salted caramel and chocolate brownie ice creams soften. Spread a layer of salted caramel ice cream over the crust, followed by a layer of chocolate brownie ice cream.
3. **Freeze**: Smooth the top and freeze for at least 4 hours or overnight.
4. **Serve**: Top with whipped cream, drizzle with caramel sauce, and sprinkle with sea salt before serving.

Pumpkin Spice Ice Cream Cake

Ingredients:

- 1 pint pumpkin ice cream
- 1 pint vanilla ice cream
- 1 1/2 cups graham cracker crumbs
- 1/4 cup unsalted butter, melted
- 1/2 teaspoon pumpkin spice
- 1/2 cup whipped cream
- Cinnamon (for garnish)

Instructions:

1. **Prepare the crust**: Combine graham cracker crumbs with melted butter and press into the bottom of a 9-inch springform pan. Freeze for 15-20 minutes.
2. **Layer ice cream**: Let the pumpkin and vanilla ice creams soften. Mix pumpkin spice into the pumpkin ice cream and spread a layer of pumpkin ice cream over the crust, followed by a layer of vanilla ice cream.
3. **Freeze**: Smooth the top and freeze for at least 4 hours or overnight.
4. **Serve**: Top with whipped cream and sprinkle with cinnamon before serving.

Chocolate Hazelnut Ice Cream Cake

Ingredients:

- 1 pint chocolate hazelnut ice cream
- 1 pint vanilla ice cream
- 1 1/2 cups crushed chocolate wafer cookies
- 1/4 cup unsalted butter, melted
- 1/2 cup crushed hazelnuts
- 1/4 cup chocolate syrup (optional)

Instructions:

1. **Make the crust**: Combine crushed chocolate wafer cookies with melted butter and press into the bottom of a 9-inch springform pan. Freeze for 15-20 minutes.
2. **Layer ice cream**: Let the chocolate hazelnut and vanilla ice creams soften. Spread a layer of chocolate hazelnut ice cream over the crust, followed by a layer of vanilla ice cream.
3. **Freeze**: Smooth the top and freeze for at least 4 hours or overnight.
4. **Serve**: Top with whipped cream, sprinkle with crushed hazelnuts, and drizzle with chocolate syrup if desired.

Dulce de Leche Ice Cream Cake

Ingredients:

- 1 pint dulce de leche ice cream
- 1 pint vanilla ice cream
- 1 1/2 cups crushed graham crackers
- 1/4 cup unsalted butter, melted
- 1/2 cup dulce de leche sauce
- 1/2 cup whipped cream

Instructions:

1. **Prepare the crust**: Mix graham cracker crumbs with melted butter and press into the bottom of a 9-inch springform pan. Freeze for 15-20 minutes.
2. **Layer ice cream**: Let the dulce de leche and vanilla ice creams soften. Spread a layer of dulce de leche ice cream over the crust, followed by a layer of vanilla ice cream.
3. **Freeze**: Smooth the top and freeze for at least 4 hours or overnight.
4. **Serve**: Top with whipped cream and drizzle with dulce de leche sauce before serving.

Apple Pie Ice Cream Cake

Ingredients:

- 1 pint cinnamon ice cream
- 1 pint vanilla ice cream
- 1 1/2 cups graham cracker crumbs
- 1/4 cup unsalted butter, melted
- 1 cup cooked and chopped apples (cinnamon-flavored)
- 1/2 cup whipped cream
- Cinnamon sugar (for garnish)

Instructions:

1. **Make the crust**: Combine graham cracker crumbs with melted butter and press into the bottom of a 9-inch springform pan. Freeze for 15-20 minutes.
2. **Layer ice cream**: Let the cinnamon and vanilla ice creams soften. Spread a layer of cinnamon ice cream over the crust, followed by a layer of vanilla ice cream.
3. **Freeze**: Smooth the top and freeze for at least 4 hours or overnight.
4. **Serve**: Top with whipped cream, chopped apples, and a sprinkle of cinnamon sugar before serving.

Blueberry Cheesecake Ice Cream Cake

Ingredients:

- 1 pint blueberry cheesecake ice cream
- 1 pint vanilla ice cream
- 1 1/2 cups graham cracker crumbs
- 1/4 cup unsalted butter, melted
- 1/2 cup fresh blueberries (optional)
- 1/2 cup whipped cream

Instructions:

1. **Prepare the crust**: Combine graham cracker crumbs with melted butter and press into the bottom of a 9-inch springform pan. Freeze for 15-20 minutes.
2. **Layer ice cream**: Let the blueberry cheesecake and vanilla ice creams soften. Spread a layer of blueberry cheesecake ice cream over the crust, followed by a layer of vanilla ice cream.
3. **Freeze**: Smooth the top and freeze for at least 4 hours or overnight.
4. **Serve**: Top with whipped cream and fresh blueberries before serving.

Chocolate Mint Chip Ice Cream Cake

Ingredients:

- 1 pint mint chocolate chip ice cream
- 1 pint chocolate ice cream
- 1 1/2 cups chocolate cookie crumbs
- 1/4 cup unsalted butter, melted
- 1/2 cup whipped cream
- Chocolate chips or shaved chocolate (optional for garnish)

Instructions:

1. **Make the crust**: Combine chocolate cookie crumbs with melted butter and press into the bottom of a 9-inch springform pan. Freeze for 15-20 minutes.
2. **Layer ice cream**: Let the mint chocolate chip and chocolate ice creams soften. Spread a layer of mint chocolate chip ice cream over the crust, followed by a layer of chocolate ice cream.
3. **Freeze**: Smooth the top and freeze for at least 4 hours or overnight.
4. **Serve**: Top with whipped cream and garnish with chocolate chips or shaved chocolate.

Almond Joy Ice Cream Cake

Ingredients:

- 1 pint coconut ice cream
- 1 pint chocolate ice cream
- 1 1/2 cups crushed chocolate almond joy bars (or similar)
- 1/4 cup unsalted butter, melted
- 1/2 cup whipped cream
- Shaved almonds (for garnish)

Instructions:

1. **Prepare the crust**: Mix crushed almond joy bars with melted butter and press into the bottom of a 9-inch springform pan. Freeze for 15-20 minutes.
2. **Layer ice cream**: Let the coconut and chocolate ice creams soften. Spread a layer of coconut ice cream over the crust, followed by a layer of chocolate ice cream.
3. **Freeze**: Smooth the top and freeze for at least 4 hours or overnight.
4. **Serve**: Top with whipped cream and garnish with shaved almonds.

Pina Colada Ice Cream Cake

Ingredients:

- 1 pint coconut ice cream
- 1 pint pineapple ice cream
- 1 1/2 cups crushed graham crackers
- 1/4 cup unsalted butter, melted
- 1/2 cup shredded coconut
- 1/4 cup rum (optional)
- Pineapple slices (for garnish)

Instructions:

1. **Make the crust**: Combine crushed graham crackers with melted butter and press into the bottom of a 9-inch springform pan. Freeze for 15-20 minutes.
2. **Layer ice cream**: Let the coconut and pineapple ice creams soften. Spread a layer of coconut ice cream over the crust, followed by a layer of pineapple ice cream.
3. **Freeze**: Smooth the top and freeze for at least 4 hours or overnight.
4. **Serve**: Garnish with shredded coconut and pineapple slices. Optionally drizzle with rum before serving.

Raspberry Truffle Ice Cream Cake

Ingredients:

- 1 pint raspberry sorbet
- 1 pint chocolate ice cream
- 1 1/2 cups chocolate wafer crumbs
- 1/4 cup unsalted butter, melted
- 1/2 cup mini chocolate chips
- Fresh raspberries (for garnish)

Instructions:

1. **Prepare the crust**: Combine chocolate wafer crumbs with melted butter and press into the bottom of a 9-inch springform pan. Freeze for 15-20 minutes.
2. **Layer ice cream**: Let the raspberry sorbet and chocolate ice cream soften. Spread a layer of raspberry sorbet over the crust, followed by a layer of chocolate ice cream.
3. **Freeze**: Smooth the top and freeze for at least 4 hours or overnight.
4. **Serve**: Top with mini chocolate chips and fresh raspberries before serving.

Tiramisu Ice Cream Cake with Espresso Crunch

Ingredients:

- 1 pint coffee ice cream
- 1 pint vanilla ice cream
- 1 1/2 cups crushed ladyfingers
- 1/4 cup espresso, cooled
- 1/2 cup whipped cream
- Cocoa powder (for garnish)

Instructions:

1. **Make the crust**: Dip ladyfingers in cooled espresso and layer them on the bottom of a 9-inch springform pan. Freeze for 15-20 minutes.
2. **Layer ice cream**: Let the coffee and vanilla ice creams soften. Spread a layer of coffee ice cream over the ladyfingers, followed by a layer of vanilla ice cream.
3. **Freeze**: Smooth the top and freeze for at least 4 hours or overnight.
4. **Serve**: Top with whipped cream and dust with cocoa powder before serving.

Lemon Blueberry Ice Cream Cake

Ingredients:

- 1 pint lemon ice cream
- 1 pint blueberry ice cream
- 1 1/2 cups graham cracker crumbs
- 1/4 cup unsalted butter, melted
- 1/2 cup fresh blueberries
- Lemon zest (for garnish)

Instructions:

1. **Make the crust**: Combine graham cracker crumbs with melted butter and press into the bottom of a 9-inch springform pan. Freeze for 15-20 minutes.
2. **Layer ice cream**: Let the lemon and blueberry ice creams soften. Spread a layer of lemon ice cream over the crust, followed by a layer of blueberry ice cream.
3. **Freeze**: Smooth the top and freeze for at least 4 hours or overnight.
4. **Serve**: Top with fresh blueberries and garnish with lemon zest before serving.

Birthday Cake Ice Cream Cake

Ingredients:

- 1 pint funfetti ice cream
- 1 pint vanilla ice cream
- 1 1/2 cups crushed confetti cake
- 1/4 cup unsalted butter, melted
- 1/2 cup whipped cream
- Sprinkles (for garnish)

Instructions:

1. **Prepare the crust**: Combine crushed confetti cake with melted butter and press into the bottom of a 9-inch springform pan. Freeze for 15-20 minutes.
2. **Layer ice cream**: Let the funfetti and vanilla ice creams soften. Spread a layer of funfetti ice cream over the crust, followed by a layer of vanilla ice cream.
3. **Freeze**: Smooth the top and freeze for at least 4 hours or overnight.
4. **Serve**: Top with whipped cream and sprinkles before serving.

Chocolate Raspberry Ice Cream Cake

Ingredients:

- 1 pint raspberry sorbet
- 1 pint chocolate ice cream
- 1 1/2 cups chocolate cookie crumbs
- 1/4 cup unsalted butter, melted
- 1/2 cup fresh raspberries
- Chocolate ganache (for drizzling)

Instructions:

1. **Make the crust**: Combine chocolate cookie crumbs with melted butter and press into the bottom of a 9-inch springform pan. Freeze for 15-20 minutes.
2. **Layer ice cream**: Let the raspberry sorbet and chocolate ice cream soften. Spread a layer of raspberry sorbet over the crust, followed by a layer of chocolate ice cream.
3. **Freeze**: Smooth the top and freeze for at least 4 hours or overnight.
4. **Serve**: Top with fresh raspberries and drizzle with chocolate ganache before serving.

Coffee Toffee Ice Cream Cake

Ingredients:

- 1 pint coffee ice cream
- 1 pint vanilla ice cream
- 1 1/2 cups crushed toffee bars
- 1/4 cup unsalted butter, melted
- 1/2 cup whipped cream
- Chopped toffee bars (for garnish)

Instructions:

1. **Make the crust**: Combine crushed toffee bars with melted butter and press into the bottom of a 9-inch springform pan. Freeze for 15-20 minutes.
2. **Layer ice cream**: Let the coffee and vanilla ice creams soften. Spread a layer of coffee ice cream over the crust, followed by a layer of vanilla ice cream.
3. **Freeze**: Smooth the top and freeze for at least 4 hours or overnight.
4. **Serve**: Top with whipped cream and garnish with chopped toffee bars before serving.

Peanut Butter Banana Ice Cream Cake

Ingredients:

- 1 pint peanut butter ice cream
- 1 pint banana ice cream
- 1 1/2 cups graham cracker crumbs
- 1/4 cup unsalted butter, melted
- 1/2 cup chopped bananas
- 1/4 cup peanut butter (for drizzling)

Instructions:

1. **Make the crust**: Combine graham cracker crumbs with melted butter and press into the bottom of a 9-inch springform pan. Freeze for 15-20 minutes.
2. **Layer ice cream**: Let the peanut butter and banana ice creams soften. Spread a layer of peanut butter ice cream over the crust, followed by a layer of banana ice cream.
3. **Freeze**: Smooth the top and freeze for at least 4 hours or overnight.
4. **Serve**: Top with chopped bananas and drizzle with peanut butter before serving.

Pistachio Almond Ice Cream Cake

Ingredients:

- 1 pint pistachio ice cream
- 1 pint vanilla ice cream
- 1 1/2 cups crushed pistachios
- 1/4 cup unsalted butter, melted
- 1/2 cup whipped cream
- Sliced almonds (for garnish)

Instructions:

1. **Prepare the crust**: Combine crushed pistachios with melted butter and press into the bottom of a 9-inch springform pan. Freeze for 15-20 minutes.
2. **Layer ice cream**: Let the pistachio and vanilla ice creams soften. Spread a layer of pistachio ice cream over the crust, followed by a layer of vanilla ice cream.
3. **Freeze**: Smooth the top and freeze for at least 4 hours or overnight.
4. **Serve**: Top with whipped cream and garnish with sliced almonds before serving.

Chocolate Cherry Ice Cream Cake

Ingredients:

- 1 pint cherry ice cream
- 1 pint chocolate ice cream
- 1 1/2 cups crushed chocolate graham crackers
- 1/4 cup unsalted butter, melted
- 1/2 cup maraschino cherries (chopped)
- Chocolate syrup (for drizzling)

Instructions:

1. **Make the crust**: Combine chocolate graham cracker crumbs with melted butter and press into the bottom of a 9-inch springform pan. Freeze for 15-20 minutes.
2. **Layer ice cream**: Let the cherry and chocolate ice creams soften. Spread a layer of cherry ice cream over the crust, followed by a layer of chocolate ice cream.
3. **Freeze**: Smooth the top and freeze for at least 4 hours or overnight.
4. **Serve**: Top with chopped maraschino cherries and drizzle with chocolate syrup.

Mango Coconut Ice Cream Cake

Ingredients:

- 1 pint mango sorbet
- 1 pint coconut ice cream
- 1 1/2 cups graham cracker crumbs
- 1/4 cup unsalted butter, melted
- 1/2 cup shredded coconut
- Mango slices (for garnish)

Instructions:

1. **Prepare the crust**: Combine graham cracker crumbs with melted butter and press into the bottom of a 9-inch springform pan. Freeze for 15-20 minutes.
2. **Layer ice cream**: Let the mango sorbet and coconut ice cream soften. Spread a layer of mango sorbet over the crust, followed by a layer of coconut ice cream.
3. **Freeze**: Smooth the top and freeze for at least 4 hours or overnight.
4. **Serve**: Garnish with shredded coconut and mango slices before serving.

Key Lime Pie Ice Cream Cake

Ingredients:

- 1 pint key lime pie ice cream
- 1 pint vanilla ice cream
- 1 1/2 cups graham cracker crumbs
- 1/4 cup unsalted butter, melted
- 1/2 cup whipped cream
- Lime zest (for garnish)

Instructions:

1. **Prepare the crust**: Combine graham cracker crumbs with melted butter and press into the bottom of a 9-inch springform pan. Freeze for 15-20 minutes.
2. **Layer ice cream**: Let the key lime pie and vanilla ice creams soften. Spread a layer of key lime pie ice cream over the crust, followed by a layer of vanilla ice cream.
3. **Freeze**: Smooth the top and freeze for at least 4 hours or overnight.
4. **Serve**: Top with whipped cream and garnish with lime zest before serving.

Nutella Hazelnut Ice Cream Cake

Ingredients:

- 1 pint Nutella ice cream
- 1 pint hazelnut ice cream
- 1 1/2 cups crushed hazelnuts
- 1/4 cup unsalted butter, melted
- 1/2 cup Nutella (for drizzling)
- Chopped hazelnuts (for garnish)

Instructions:

1. **Make the crust**: Combine crushed hazelnuts with melted butter and press into the bottom of a 9-inch springform pan. Freeze for 15-20 minutes.
2. **Layer ice cream**: Let the Nutella and hazelnut ice creams soften. Spread a layer of Nutella ice cream over the crust, followed by a layer of hazelnut ice cream.
3. **Freeze**: Smooth the top and freeze for at least 4 hours or overnight.
4. **Serve**: Drizzle with Nutella and garnish with chopped hazelnuts before serving.

Oreo Truffle Ice Cream Cake

Ingredients:

- 1 pint cookies and cream ice cream
- 1 pint vanilla ice cream
- 1 1/2 cups crushed Oreo cookies
- 1/4 cup unsalted butter, melted
- 1/2 cup chocolate ganache
- Whole Oreos (for garnish)

Instructions:

1. **Prepare the crust**: Combine crushed Oreos with melted butter and press into the bottom of a 9-inch springform pan. Freeze for 15-20 minutes.
2. **Layer ice cream**: Let the cookies and cream and vanilla ice creams soften. Spread a layer of cookies and cream ice cream over the crust, followed by a layer of vanilla ice cream.
3. **Freeze**: Smooth the top and freeze for at least 4 hours or overnight.
4. **Serve**: Top with chocolate ganache and garnish with whole Oreos.

Maple Pecan Ice Cream Cake

Ingredients:

- 1 pint maple ice cream
- 1 pint vanilla ice cream
- 1 1/2 cups chopped pecans
- 1/4 cup unsalted butter, melted
- 1/2 cup caramel sauce
- Toasted pecans (for garnish)

Instructions:

1. **Make the crust**: Combine chopped pecans with melted butter and press into the bottom of a 9-inch springform pan. Freeze for 15-20 minutes.
2. **Layer ice cream**: Let the maple and vanilla ice creams soften. Spread a layer of maple ice cream over the crust, followed by a layer of vanilla ice cream.
3. **Freeze**: Smooth the top and freeze for at least 4 hours or overnight.
4. **Serve**: Drizzle with caramel sauce and garnish with toasted pecans before serving.

Banana Foster Ice Cream Cake

Ingredients:

- 1 pint banana ice cream
- 1 pint vanilla ice cream
- 1 1/2 cups crushed graham crackers
- 1/4 cup unsalted butter, melted
- 1/2 cup dark rum
- 1/2 cup sliced bananas (for garnish)

Instructions:

1. **Make the crust**: Combine crushed graham crackers with melted butter and press into the bottom of a 9-inch springform pan. Freeze for 15-20 minutes.
2. **Layer ice cream**: Let the banana and vanilla ice creams soften. Spread a layer of banana ice cream over the crust, followed by a layer of vanilla ice cream.
3. **Freeze**: Smooth the top and freeze for at least 4 hours or overnight.
4. **Serve**: Drizzle with dark rum and garnish with sliced bananas before serving.

Chocolate Chip Cookie Dough Ice Cream Cake

Ingredients:

- 1 pint chocolate chip cookie dough ice cream
- 1 pint vanilla ice cream
- 1 1/2 cups crushed chocolate chip cookies
- 1/4 cup unsalted butter, melted
- 1/2 cup chocolate chips
- Whipped cream (for garnish)

Instructions:

1. **Prepare the crust**: Combine crushed chocolate chip cookies with melted butter and press into the bottom of a 9-inch springform pan. Freeze for 15-20 minutes.
2. **Layer ice cream**: Let the chocolate chip cookie dough and vanilla ice creams soften. Spread a layer of chocolate chip cookie dough ice cream over the crust, followed by a layer of vanilla ice cream.
3. **Freeze**: Smooth the top and freeze for at least 4 hours or overnight.
4. **Serve**: Top with whipped cream and chocolate chips before serving.

Chocolate Coconut Ice Cream Cake

Ingredients:

- 1 pint chocolate ice cream
- 1 pint coconut ice cream
- 1 1/2 cups chocolate graham cracker crumbs
- 1/4 cup unsalted butter, melted
- 1/2 cup shredded coconut
- Chocolate syrup (for drizzling)

Instructions:

1. **Make the crust**: Combine chocolate graham cracker crumbs with melted butter and press into the bottom of a 9-inch springform pan. Freeze for 15-20 minutes.
2. **Layer ice cream**: Let the chocolate and coconut ice creams soften. Spread a layer of chocolate ice cream over the crust, followed by a layer of coconut ice cream.
3. **Freeze**: Smooth the top and freeze for at least 4 hours or overnight.
4. **Serve**: Top with shredded coconut and drizzle with chocolate syrup.

Cherry Almond Ice Cream Cake

Ingredients:

- 1 pint cherry ice cream
- 1 pint almond ice cream
- 1 1/2 cups crushed almonds
- 1/4 cup unsalted butter, melted
- 1/2 cup cherry topping
- Chopped almonds (for garnish)

Instructions:

1. **Make the crust**: Combine crushed almonds with melted butter and press into the bottom of a 9-inch springform pan. Freeze for 15-20 minutes.
2. **Layer ice cream**: Let the cherry and almond ice creams soften. Spread a layer of cherry ice cream over the crust, followed by a layer of almond ice cream.
3. **Freeze**: Smooth the top and freeze for at least 4 hours or overnight.
4. **Serve**: Top with cherry topping and garnish with chopped almonds.

Carrot Cake Ice Cream Cake

Ingredients:

- 1 pint carrot cake ice cream
- 1 pint vanilla ice cream
- 1 1/2 cups crushed walnuts
- 1/4 cup unsalted butter, melted
- 1/2 cup cream cheese frosting
- Walnuts (for garnish)

Instructions:

1. **Make the crust**: Combine crushed walnuts with melted butter and press into the bottom of a 9-inch springform pan. Freeze for 15-20 minutes.
2. **Layer ice cream**: Let the carrot cake and vanilla ice creams soften. Spread a layer of carrot cake ice cream over the crust, followed by a layer of vanilla ice cream.
3. **Freeze**: Smooth the top and freeze for at least 4 hours or overnight.
4. **Serve**: Top with cream cheese frosting and garnish with walnuts.

Cookies and Caramel Ice Cream Cake

Ingredients:

- 1 pint caramel ice cream
- 1 pint cookies and cream ice cream
- 1 1/2 cups crushed chocolate chip cookies
- 1/4 cup unsalted butter, melted
- 1/2 cup caramel sauce
- Whipped cream (for garnish)

Instructions:

1. **Prepare the crust**: Combine crushed cookies with melted butter and press into the bottom of a 9-inch springform pan. Freeze for 15-20 minutes.
2. **Layer ice cream**: Let the caramel and cookies and cream ice creams soften. Spread a layer of caramel ice cream over the crust, followed by a layer of cookies and cream ice cream.
3. **Freeze**: Smooth the top and freeze for at least 4 hours or overnight.
4. **Serve**: Drizzle with caramel sauce and top with whipped cream before serving.

Tropical Paradise Ice Cream Cake

Ingredients:

- 1 pint coconut ice cream
- 1 pint mango sorbet
- 1 1/2 cups crushed graham crackers
- 1/4 cup unsalted butter, melted
- 1/2 cup shredded coconut
- Tropical fruit slices (for garnish)

Instructions:

1. **Make the crust**: Combine crushed graham crackers with melted butter and press into the bottom of a 9-inch springform pan. Freeze for 15-20 minutes.
2. **Layer ice cream**: Let the coconut ice cream and mango sorbet soften. Spread a layer of coconut ice cream over the crust, followed by a layer of mango sorbet.
3. **Freeze**: Smooth the top and freeze for at least 4 hours or overnight.
4. **Serve**: Top with shredded coconut and tropical fruit slices before serving.

Triple Chocolate Ice Cream Cake

Ingredients:

- 1 pint chocolate ice cream
- 1 pint chocolate fudge ice cream
- 1 pint chocolate chip ice cream
- 1 1/2 cups chocolate wafer crumbs
- 1/4 cup unsalted butter, melted
- 1/2 cup chocolate ganache
- Chocolate shavings (for garnish)

Instructions:

1. **Prepare the crust**: Combine chocolate wafer crumbs with melted butter and press into the bottom of a 9-inch springform pan. Freeze for 15-20 minutes.
2. **Layer ice cream**: Let the chocolate ice cream, chocolate fudge ice cream, and chocolate chip ice cream soften. Spread a layer of chocolate ice cream over the crust, followed by a layer of chocolate fudge ice cream and then chocolate chip ice cream.
3. **Freeze**: Smooth the top and freeze for at least 4 hours or overnight.
4. **Serve**: Drizzle with chocolate ganache and garnish with chocolate shavings before serving.

Vanilla Almond Crunch Ice Cream Cake

Ingredients:

- 1 pint vanilla ice cream
- 1 pint almond ice cream
- 1 1/2 cups crushed almond cookies
- 1/4 cup unsalted butter, melted
- 1/2 cup sliced almonds
- Honey (for drizzling)

Instructions:

1. **Prepare the crust**: Combine crushed almond cookies with melted butter and press into the bottom of a 9-inch springform pan. Freeze for 15-20 minutes.
2. **Layer ice cream**: Let the vanilla and almond ice creams soften. Spread a layer of vanilla ice cream over the crust, followed by a layer of almond ice cream.
3. **Freeze**: Smooth the top and freeze for at least 4 hours or overnight.
4. **Serve**: Top with sliced almonds and drizzle with honey before serving.

Raspberry Lemonade Ice Cream Cake

Ingredients:

- 1 pint raspberry sorbet
- 1 pint lemonade ice cream
- 1 1/2 cups graham cracker crumbs
- 1/4 cup unsalted butter, melted
- 1/2 cup fresh raspberries
- Lemon zest (for garnish)

Instructions:

1. **Make the crust**: Combine graham cracker crumbs with melted butter and press into the bottom of a 9-inch springform pan. Freeze for 15-20 minutes.
2. **Layer ice cream**: Let the raspberry sorbet and lemonade ice cream soften. Spread a layer of raspberry sorbet over the crust, followed by a layer of lemonade ice cream.
3. **Freeze**: Smooth the top and freeze for at least 4 hours or overnight.
4. **Serve**: Top with fresh raspberries and garnish with lemon zest before serving.

Mocha Hazelnut Ice Cream Cake

Ingredients:

- 1 pint mocha ice cream
- 1 pint hazelnut ice cream

- 1 1/2 cups crushed biscotti
- 1/4 cup unsalted butter, melted
- 1/2 cup hazelnut spread (for drizzling)
- Chopped hazelnuts (for garnish)

Instructions:

1. **Make the crust**: Combine crushed biscotti with melted butter and press into the bottom of a 9-inch springform pan. Freeze for 15-20 minutes.
2. **Layer ice cream**: Let the mocha and hazelnut ice creams soften. Spread a layer of mocha ice cream over the crust, followed by a layer of hazelnut ice cream.
3. **Freeze**: Smooth the top and freeze for at least 4 hours or overnight.
4. **Serve**: Drizzle with hazelnut spread and garnish with chopped hazelnuts before serving.

Chocolate-Covered Strawberry Ice Cream Cake

Ingredients:

- 1 pint strawberry ice cream
- 1 pint chocolate ice cream
- 1 1/2 cups chocolate cookie crumbs
- 1/4 cup unsalted butter, melted
- 1/2 cup chocolate ganache
- Fresh strawberries (for garnish)

Instructions:

1. **Prepare the crust**: Combine chocolate cookie crumbs with melted butter and press into the bottom of a 9-inch springform pan. Freeze for 15-20 minutes.
2. **Layer ice cream**: Let the strawberry and chocolate ice creams soften. Spread a layer of strawberry ice cream over the crust, followed by a layer of chocolate ice cream.
3. **Freeze**: Smooth the top and freeze for at least 4 hours or overnight.
4. **Serve**: Drizzle with chocolate ganache and garnish with fresh strawberries before serving.

www.ingramcontent.com/pod-product-compliance
Lightning Source LLC
LaVergne TN
LVHW081500060526
838201LV00056BA/2850